Bright Star Shining

This selection and arrangement copyright © 1993 by
Michael Harrison and Christopher Stuart-Clark

First published in 1993 by Oxford University Press

This edition published in 1998 by
Eerdmans Books for Young Readers
an imprint of
William B. Eerdmans Publishing Company
255 Jefferson Ave. S.E., Grand Rapids, Michigan 49503 /
P.O. Box 163, Cambridge CB3 9PU U.K.
Printed in Hong Kong

03 02 01 00 99 98   7 6 5 4 3 2 1

Library of Congress Cataloging-in-Publication Data

Bright star shining: poems for Christmas / selected by
Michael Harrison and Christopher Stuart-Clark.
p.   cm.
Originally published: Oxford: Oxford University Press, 1993.
Includes index.
ISBN 0-8028-5177-0 (alk. paper)
1. Christmas — Poetry.
I. Harrison, Michael, 1939- .
II. Stuart-Clark, Christopher.
PN6110.C5B665   1988
808.81'9334 — dc21   98-7788
CIP

BRIGHT STAR
SHINING

Poems for Christmas

Selected by
Michael Harrison and Christopher Stuart-Clark

Eerdmans Books for Young Readers
Grand Rapids, Michigan / Cambridge, U.K.

Contents

From "The Star of the Nativity"

It was wintertime.
The wind was blowing from the plains.
And the infant was cold in the cave
On the slope of a hill.

He was warmed by the breath of an ox.
Every farmyard beast
Huddled safe in the cave;
A warm mist drifted over the manger.

On a rock afar some drowsy shepherds
Shook off the wisps of straw
And hayseed of their beds,
And sleepily gazed into the vast of night.

One star alone
Unseen until then
Shone bright on the way to Bethlehem.

"Let us go and worship the miracle,"
They said, and belted their sheepskin coats.

Their bodies grew warm, walking through snows.
There were footprints that glinted like mica
Across bright fields, on the way to the inn.

The frosty night was like a fairy tale.
The dogs grew fearful
And huddled beside the shepherd lads.

He slept in His manger in radiant light,
As a moonbeam sleeps in a hollow tree.
The breath of the ox and the ass kept warm
His hands and feet in the cold of night.

Boris Pasternak   *Translated by Eugene Kayden*

Shepherds' Song

High in the heaven
A gold star burns
Lighting our way
As the great world turns.

Silver the frost
It shines on the stem
As we now journey
To Bethlehem.

White is the ice
At our feet as we tread,
Pointing a path
To the manger-bed.

Charles Causley

The Shepherd's Dog

Out on the windy hill
Under that sudden star
A blaze of radiant light
Frightened my master.

He got up, left our sheep,
Tramped over the moor.
And I, following,
Came to this open door,

Sidled in, settled down,
Head on my paws,
Glad to be here, away
From the wind's sharpness.

Such warmth is in this shed,
Such comfort from this Child,
That I forget my hard life,
Ignore the harsh world,

And see on my master's face
The same joy I possess,
The knowledge of peace,
True happiness.

Leslie Norris

Room at the Inn

Drafty, husband, that stable.
She looked . . . warm, though.
Almost at home.
And you know, husband, I swear
it's not one mite as dark in there
as you'd have thought.
And that child—so still, so quiet.
Perhaps they'll need more straw?
It won't get any warmer, early hours.
Maybe we should bring them in?
Husband, you're not listening!

There is our bed . . .
but then with breakfast early
and so many travelers . . .
Well, *they* won't go tomorrow, surely?
Husband, did you see . . . ?
Husband!
Oh well, old man, dream on!
Some day we've had,
and then those two arriving,
with every nook and cranny gone!

Funny how those moths
circled the old lantern,
husband. Almost like . . .
almost as if those three . . .
but no, it couldn't be!
And the light,
you should have seen the light!
Oh, it flickered, but
so bright, so bright,
and night so still.
Drafty it is, that stable,
husband.

Judith Nicholls

Mary's Song

Sleep, King Jesus,
Your royal bed
Is made of hay
In a cattle-shed.
Sleep, King Jesus,
Do not fear,
Joseph is watching
And waiting near.

Warm in the wintry air
You lie,
The ox and the donkey
Standing by,
With summer eyes
They seem to say:
Welcome, Jesus,
On Christmas Day!

Sleep, King Jesus:
Your diamond crown
High in the sky
Where the stars look down.
Let your reign
Of love begin,
That all the world
May enter in.

Charles Causley

Carol of the Field Mice

Villagers all, this frosty tide,
Let your doors swing open wide,
Though wind may follow, and snow beside,
Yet draw us in by your fire to bide,
　　Joy shall be yours in the morning!

Here we stand in the cold and the sleet,
Blowing fingers and stamping feet,
Come from far away you to greet—
You by the fire and we in the street—
　　Bidding you joy in the morning!

For ere one half of the night was gone,
Sudden a star has led us on,
Raining bliss and benison—
Bliss tomorrow and more anon,
　　Joy for every morning!

Goodman Joseph toiled through the snow—
Saw the star o'er a stable low;
Mary she might not further go—
Welcome thatch, and litter below!
　　Joy was hers in the morning!

And then they heard the angels tell,
"Who were the first to cry Noel?
Animals all, as it befell,
In the stable where they did dwell!
　　Joy shall be theirs in the morning!"

Kenneth Grahame

A Christmas Folk Song

The little Jesus came to town;
The wind blew up, the wind blew down;
Out in the street the wind was bold;
Now who would house Him from the cold?

Then opened wide a stable door,
Fair were the rushes on the floor;
The Ox put forth a hornèd head:
"Come, Little Lord, here make Thy bed."

Up rose the Sheep were folded near:
"Thou Lamb of God, come, enter here."
He entered there to rush and reed,
Who was the Lamb of God indeed.

The little Jesus came to town;
With ox and sheep He laid Him down;
Peace to the byre, peace to the fold,
For that they housed Him from the cold!

Lizette Woodworth Reese

Stable Song

She lies, a stillness in the crumpled straw
Whilst he looks softly on the child, unsure,
And shadows waver by the stable door.

The oxen stir; a moth drifts through the bare
Outbuilding, silken Gabriel-winged, to where
She lies, a stillness in the crumpled straw.

A carpenter, his wife, both unaware
That kings and shepherds seek them from afar
And shadows waver by the stable door.

The child sleeps on. A drowse of asses snore;
He murmurs gently, raises eyes to her
Who lies, a stillness in the crumpled straw.

A cockerel crows, disturbed by sudden fear
As shepherds, dark upon the hill, appear
And shadows waver by the stable door.

The hush of birth is in the midnight air
And new life hides the distant smell of myrrh;
She lies, a stillness in the crumpled straw,
And shadows waver by the stable door.

Judith Nicholls

The First Christmas

A star was His night-light
His quilt was the sky,
And soft sang His mother
In case He should cry;
And all the brown cattle
Came close to His bed
To see the small Baby
Asleep in their shed.

His carols were praises
Of love and goodwill,
That rose in the midnight
So clear and so still,
To herald the earliest
Christmas we know,
When Jesus was little,
A long time ago.

Elizabeth Fleming

Christmas Morn

Shall I tell you what will come
to Bethlehem on Christmas morn,
who will kneel them gently down
before the Lord new-born?

One small fish from the river,
with scales of red, red gold,
one wild bee from the heather,
one grey lamb from the fold,
one ox from the high pasture,
one black bull from the herd,
one goatling from the far hills,
one white, white bird.

And many children—God give them grace,
bringing tall candles to light Mary's face.

Ruth Sawyer

The Riding of the Kings

In a far land upon a day,
Where never snow did fall,
Three Kings went riding on the way,
Bearing presents all.

And one wore red, and one wore gold,
And one was clad in green,
And one was young, and one was old,
And one was in between.

The middle one had human sense,
The young had loving eyes,
The old had much experience,
And all of them were wise.

Choosing no guide by eve and morn
But heaven's starry drifts,
They rode to find the Newly-Born
For whom they carried gifts.

Oh, far away in time they rode
Upon their wanderings,
And still in story goes abroad
The riding of the Kings:

So wise, that in their chosen hour,
As through the world they filed,
They sought not wealth or place or power,
But rode to find a Child.

Eleanor Farjeon

We Three Camels

I carried a king,
But not the Child,
Through desert storms
And winds so wild
The sands crept into
Every pack.
But never did
My king look back.
"Forward!" he cried.
"We follow the star.
We do not stop."
So here we are.

I carried a king,
But not the One,
Through searing heat
And blinding sun,
Through nights so cold
My nostrils froze,
And slaves wrapped cloths
About my toes.
But forward we went
Led by a star.
We did not stop,
So here we are.

I carried a king,
But not the Babe,
And also boxes
Jewel inlaid.
My packs were stuffed
With scents and spice,
The grandest ladies
To entice.
No ladies saw we,
But only a star.
We did not stop,
So here we are.

Jane Yolen

The Donkey's Song

I was cradle and crib
Before the manger.
I was guardian and guard
Against all danger.
I was rocker and rock,
I was God's own cart,
I was breath against cold,
I was His strong heart.

Jane Yolen

Nativity Play

This year . . .
This year can I be Herod?
This year, can I be him?
A wise man
or a Joseph?
An inn man
or a king?

This year . . .
can I be famous?
This year, can I be best?
Bear a crown of silver
and wear a golden vest?

This year . . .
can I be starlight?
This year, can I stand out?

. . . feel the swish of curtains
and hear the front row shout
"Hurrah" for good old Ronny.
He brings a gift of gold,
head afire with tinsel—
"The Greatest Story Told . . ."

So—
don't make me a palm tree
And can I be—
                                    a Star?

Peter Dixon

Keeping Christmas

How will you your Christmas keep?
Feasting, fasting, or asleep?
Will you laugh or will you pray,
Or will you forget the day?

Be it kept with joy or prayer,
Keep of either some to spare;
Whatsoever brings the day,
Do not keep but give away.

Eleanor Farjeon

little tree

little tree
little silent Christmas tree
you are so little
you are more like a flower

who found you in the green forest
and were you very sorry to come away?
see i will comfort you
because you smell so sweetly

i will kiss your cool bark
and hug you safe and tight
just as your mother would,
only don't be afraid

look the spangles
that sleep all the year in a dark box
dreaming of being taken out and allowed to shine,
the balls the chains red and gold the fluffy threads,

put up your little arms
and i'll give them all to you to hold
every finger shall have its ring
and there won't be a single place dark or unhappy

then when you're quite dressed
you'll stand in the window for everyone to see
and how they'll stare!
oh but you'll be very proud

and my little sister and i will take hands
and looking up at our beautiful tree
we'll dance and sing
"Noel Noel"

e e cummings

Christmas Tree

Star over all
Eye of the night
Stand on my tree
Magical sight
Green under frost
Green under snow
Green under tinsel
Glitter and glow
Appled with baubles
Silver and gold
Spangled with fire
Warm over cold.

Laurence Smith

28

Christmas Lights

Bulbs strung along
Our porch roof
Pour clear
Colors through the
Cold black air;

But our neighbors
Have a spruce, like
A huge shadow,
Full of deep blue
Mysterious stars.

Valerie Worth

29

Advice to a Child

Set your fir-tree
In a pot;
Needles green
Is all it's got.
Shut the door
And go away,
And so to sleep
Till Christmas Day.
In the morning
Seek your tree,
And you shall see
What you shall see.

Hang your stocking
By the fire,
Empty of
Your heart's desire;
Up the chimney
Say your say,
And so to sleep
Till Christmas Day.
In the morning
Draw the blind,
And you shall find
What you shall find.

Eleanor Farjeon

Mistletoe

Mistletoe new,
Mistletoe old,
Cut it down
With a knife of gold.

Mistletoe green,
Mistletoe milk,
Let it fall
On a scarf of silk.

Mistletoe from
The Christmas oak,
Keep my house
From lightning stroke.

Guard from thunder
My roof-tree
And any evil
That there be.

Charles Causley

Robin's Song

Robins sang in England,
Frost or rain or snow,
All the long December days
Endless years ago.

Robins sang in England
Before the Legions came,
Before our English fields were tilled
Or England was a name.

Robins sang in England
When forests dark and wild
Stretched across from sea to sea
And Jesus was a child.

Listen! in the frosty dawn
From his leafless bough
The same brave song he ever sang
A robin's singing now.

Rodney Bennett

The Christmas Mouse

A Christmas mouse
Came to our house,
Looking for crumbs
That clumsy thumbs
Had dropped on the floor.
Under the door
He quietly crept
And bits not swept
He nibbled and sniffed.
"A Christmas gift,"
Old Mousie thought
And went and brought
His relations and friends
To share the ends
Of our Christmas feast.

Daphne Lister

Unable to Sleep

Unable to sleep,
I creep downstairs;
Nothing stirs
In this room-arrested darkness.

I pull the curtain
And peep through the window;
Frost, like a memory of snow,
Whitens my garden,
The roof of my neighbor's car,
The park beyond.

The coldness of winter covers my
thoughts.

Behind me, the clock
Ticks into the ghost of time,
Ticks into my head,
Ticks into silence.

Peter Thabit Jones

Questions on Christmas Eve

But *how* can his reindeer fly without wings?
Jets on their hooves? That's plain cheating!
And *how* can he climb down the chimney pot
   When we've got central heating?

You say it's all magic and I shouldn't ask
About Santa on Christmas Eve.
But I'm confused by the stories I've heard;
   I don't know what to believe.

I said that I'd sit up in bed all night long
To see if he really would call.
But I fell fast asleep, woke up after dawn
   As something banged in the hall.

I saw my sock crammed with apples and sweets;
There were parcels piled high near the door.
Jingle bells tinkled far off in the dark;
   One snowflake shone on the floor.

Wes Magee

Mincemeat

Sing a song of mincemeat,
Currants, raisins, spice,
Apples, sugar, nutmeg,
Everything that's nice.
Stir it with a ladle,
Wish a lovely wish,
Drop it in the middle
Of your well-filled dish.
Stir again for good luck,
Pack it all away,
Tied in little jars and pots,
Until Christmas Day.

Elizabeth Gould

A Stormy Night One Christmas Day

It was a stormy night
one Christmas day
as they fell awake
on the Santa Fe.

Turkey, jelly,
and the ship's old cook
all jumped out
of a recipe book.

The jelly wobbled,
the turkey gobbled,
and after them both
the old cook hobbled.

Gobbler gobbled
Hobbler's Wobbler.
Hobbler gobbled
Wobbler's Gobbler.

Gobbly-gobbler
gobbled Wobbly.
Hobbly-hobbler
gobbled Gobbly.

Gobble gobbled
Hobble's Wobble.
Hobble gobbled
gobbled Wobble.

gobble gobble
wobble wobble
hobble gobble
wobble gobble

Michael Rosen

Country Carol

Walked on the crusted grass in the frosty air.
Blackbird saw me, gave me a gold-rimmed stare.

Walked in the winter woods where the snow lay deep.
Hedgehog heard me, smiled at me in his sleep.

Walked by the frozen pond where the ice shone pale.
Wind sang softly, moon dipped its silver sail.

Walked on the midnight hills till the star-filled dawn.
No one told me, I knew a king was born.

Sue Cowling

Snow at Christmas

God has gone berserk
  with the icing!
The marzipan is cold,
  and the cherries and nuts
    are so dark.

There's a robin
  and a snowman
next to that fir tree.
  Look! Can you see
    the postman's tracks?

Bring me a knife.
  I'm going to
cut myself a slice
  of this cake
    and eat it!

Richard Andrews

What Is Christmas?

Christmas is a lighted island
In the sea of winter darkness.

Christmas is the reindeer clatter
On the roof of the rustling house.

Christmas is the spiced kitchen
Spreading through the waiting days.

Christmas is the tongue teased
And the tummy truly tested.

Christmas is the warm hug
That wraps me in my family's love.

John Corben

Christmas Morning

If Bethlehem were here today,
Or this were very long ago,
There wouldn't be a winter time
Nor any cold or snow.

I'd run out through the garden gate,
And down along the pasture walk;
And off beside the cattle barns
I'd hear a kind of gentle talk.

I'd move the heavy iron chain
And pull away the wooden pin;
I'd push the door a little bit
And tiptoe very softly in.

The pigeons and the yellow hens
And all the cows would stand away;
Their eyes would open wide to see
A lady in the manger hay,

If this were very long ago
And Bethlehem were here today.

And Mother held my hand and smiled—
I mean the lady would—and she
Would take the woolly blankets off
Her little boy so I could see.

His shut-up eyes would be asleep,
And he would look like our John,
And he would be all crumpled too,
And have a pinkish color on.

I'd watch his breath go in and out.
His little clothes would all be white.
I'd slip my finger in his hand
To feel how he could hold it tight.

And she would smile and say, "Take care,"
The mother, Mary, would, "Take care";
And I would kiss his little hand
And touch his hair.

While Mary put the blankets back
The gentle talk would soon begin.
And when I'd tiptoe softly out
I'd meet the wise men going in.

Elizabeth Madox Roberts

A Singing in the Air

A snowy field! A stable piled
With straw! A donkey's sleepy pow!*
A Mother beaming on a Child!
A Manger, and a munching cow!
—These we all remember now—
And airy voices, heard afar!
And three Magicians, and a Star!

Two thousand times of snow declare
That on the Christmas of the year
There is a singing in the air;
And all who listen for it hear
A fairy chime, a seraph strain,
Telling He is born again,
—That all we love is born again.

James Stephens

* *pow*: head

Index of Titles and First Lines

First lines are in italics

Index of Authors

The Artists

The illustrations are by:

Stephen Lambert   pp. 6-7, 13, 20, 28-29, 39, 45

Louise Rawlings   pp. 3, 4, 5, 15, 18-19, 27, 31, 32, 33, 36, 37, 40, 41

Susan Scott   pp. 8, 9, 11, 17, 23, 24, 25, 34, 35, 42

The jacket illustrations are by *Louise Rawlings*

Acknowledgments

The editors and publisher are grateful for permission to include the following copyrighted material:

Richard Andrews: "Snow at Christmas." Reprinted in *Poetry World 2* (Bell & Hyman, an imprint of HarperCollins Publishers). **Charles Causley**: "Shepherds' Song," "Mary's Song," and "Mistletoe" from *The Gift of a Lamb: Early in the Morning* (Robson Books: Viking Kestrel). Reprinted by permission of David Higham Associates Ltd. **John Corben**: "What Is Christmas?" © John Corben 1993. Reprinted with permission. **Sue Cowling**: "Country Carol" from *What Is a Kumquat? And Other Poems*. Reprinted by permission of Faber & Faber Ltd. **e e cummings**: "little tree" from *Complete Poems of e e cummings*. Reprinted by permission of MacGibbon & Kee, an imprint of HarperCollins Publishers Limited, and Liveright Publishing Corporation. **Peter Dixon**: "Nativity Play" from *Big Billy*, © Peter Dixon 1990. Reprinted by permission of the author. **Eleanor Farjeon**: "The Riding of the Kings," "Keeping Christmas," and "Advice to a Child" from *Collected Poems*. Reprinted by permission of David Higham Associates Ltd. **Elizabeth Gould**: "Mincemeat," © Elizabeth Gould. **Peter Thabit Jones**: "Unable to Sleep." Reprinted in *A Christmas Stocking* (Cassell PLC). Reprinted by permission of the author. **Wes Magee**: "Questions on Christmas Eve," © Wes Magee, from *The Witch's Brew and Other Poems*. Reprinted by permission of the author. **Judith Nicholls**: "Room at the Inn" from *Midnight Forest and Other Poems*, and "Stable Song" from *Magic Mirror and Other Poems for Children*. Reprinted by permission of Faber & Faber Ltd. **Leslie Norris**: "The Shepherd's Dog" from *Norris's Ark* (The Tidal Press). Reprinted by permission of the author. **Elizabeth Madox Roberts**: "Christmas Morning" from *Under the Tree*, © 1922 by B. W. Huebsch, Inc., renewed 1950 by Ivor S. Roberts; © 1930 by Viking Penguin, Inc., renewed © 1958 by Ivor S. Roberts. Used by permission of Viking Penguin, a division of Penguin Books USA Inc. **Michael Rosen**: "A Stormy Night One Christmas Day" from *Mind Your Own Business*. Reprinted by permission of Scholastic Publications Ltd. **Shel Silverstein**: "Merry . . ." from *Where the Sidewalk Ends*, © 1974 by Evil Eye Music, Inc. Reprinted by permission of HarperCollins Publishers Inc., New York. **Laurence Smith**: "Christmas Tree." Reprinted by permission of the author. **James Stephens**: "A Singing in the Air." Reprinted by permission of The Society of Authors on behalf of the copyright owner, Mrs. Iris Wise. **Valerie Worth**: "Christmas Lights" from *More Small Poems*, © 1976 by Valerie Worth. Reprinted by permission of Farrar, Straus & Giroux, Inc. **Jane Yolen**: "We Three Camels" and "The Donkey's Song." Reprinted by permission of Curtis Brown, New York, for the author.

While every effort has been made to trace and contact copyright holders, this has not always been possible. If contacted, the publisher will be pleased to correct any errors or omissions at the earliest opportunity.

Merry . . .

No one's hangin' stockin's up,
No one's bakin' pie,
No one's lookin' up to see
A new star in the sky.
No one's talkin' brotherhood,
No one's givin' gifts,
And no one loves a Christmas tree
On March the twenty-fifth.

Shel Silverstein